UNIFYING AMERICA

Unifying America

Navigating the Political Terrain of Today

ANURAG ANURAG

Anurag Anurag

CONTENTS

POLITICAL POLARIZATION IN CONTEMPORARY AMERICA: A DEEPENING CHASM

Political polarization in the contemporary United States has evolved into a multifaceted challenge, deeply entrenched in the fabric of society and governance. This chapter delves into the complexities of this phenomenon, exploring its various dimensions and implications.

Political polarization has become a defining feature of American politics, characterized by a widening ideological gap between left and right. At its core, polarization reflects not only differences in policy preferences but also fundamental disparities in worldviews and values. This polarization has permeated every aspect of political discourse, hindering meaningful dialogue and compromise.

To grasp the breadth and depth of political polarization, it's essential to examine real-world examples that illustrate its impact. Imagine a scenario in which lawmakers, divided along party lines, engage in a heated debate over immigration reform. Democrats advocate for comprehensive immigration reform, emphasizing compassion and inclusivity, while Republicans push for stricter border control measures, citing concerns about national security.

The media landscape further exacerbates polarization, with news outlets catering to specific ideological leanings. Consider the contrast between a conservative-leaning outlet framing immigration as a threat to national sovereignty and a liberal-leaning outlet highlighting the humanitarian aspects of the issue. Each narrative reinforces existing beliefs, deepening the ideological divide.

The consequences of political polarization extend far beyond rhetorical battles in Washington. Legislative gridlock and governmental dysfunction have become commonplace, as lawmakers prioritize partisan interests over the common good. Imagine a scenario where a crucial piece of legislation aimed at addressing climate change languishes in Congress, with Democrats and Republicans unable to find common ground on environmental policy.

Moreover, polarization undermines public trust in institutions and erodes the foundations of democracy. Citizens increasingly view political opponents not as fellow Americans with differing perspectives but as adversaries to be defeated. This erosion of trust threatens the very fabric of society, weakening the social cohesion essential for a functioning democracy.

While the challenges posed by political polarization are daunting, there are pathways to unity and collaboration. One approach involves fostering constructive dialogue and empathy across ideological lines. Imagine a town hall meeting where citizens from diverse backgrounds come together to discuss contentious issues like healthcare and gun control, guided by principles of mutual respect and understanding.

Furthermore, promoting media literacy and critical thinking skills can help inoculate the public against the divisive effects of partisan media. Imagine a curriculum that teaches students how to evaluate sources, recognize bias, and engage critically with infor mation—a vital tool in navigating today's media landscape.

Effective leadership is essential in bridging the divides exacerbated by political polarization. Imagine a political leader who eschews partisan rhetoric in favor of inclusive language, emphasizing shared values and common goals. Such leadership sets a tone of collaboration and cooperation, inspiring others to transcend ideological differences in pursuit of the greater good.

Additionally, promoting diversity and inclusion in decision-making processes can help mitigate the effects of polarization. Imagine a corporate boardroom or legislative committee where individuals from diverse backgrounds and perspectives come together to craft innovative solutions to complex problems. By harnessing the power of diverse viewpoints, organizations can break free from the echo chambers of polarization and foster creativity and resilience.

Investing in education and civic engagement is crucial in combating political polarization. Imagine a civics curriculum that emphasizes the importance of civic responsibility, democratic values, and active citizenship. By equipping future generations with the knowledge and skills necessary to participate effectively in the political process, we can cultivate a more informed and engaged electorate, capable of bridging ideological divides.

Furthermore, encouraging grassroots activism and community organizing can empower individuals to become agents of change in their communities. Imagine a network of local organizations working together to address shared challenges, from environmental conservation to economic inequality. By mobilizing collective action at the grassroots level, communities can transcend partisan politics and effect meaningful change from the ground up.

Political polarization poses significant challenges to American democracy, threatening to undermine the principles of unity and cooperation upon which our nation was founded. However, by fostering dialogue, promoting inclusive leadership, and investing in education and civic engagement, we can begin to bridge the divides that divide us and build a more united and resilient future for all Americans.

2

THE VANISHING CENTER

The erosion of the political center in American politics is a significant phenomenon that warrants careful examination. The dwindling presence of independent voices has had profound implications for the overall political landscape, contributing to a polarized environment dominated by the binary narrative of the left and right.

The decline of independent voices can be traced back to various factors, including the increasing ideological rigidity within the major political parties. As these parties move towards more extreme positions, the space for moderates and independents shrinks, leaving voters with limited options that align with their nuanced views.

The binary narrative, characterized by the stark division between the left and right, oversimplifies complex issues and stifles the richness of diverse perspectives. This polarization not only narrows the range of policy options but also fosters a climate where compromise is often viewed as a betrayal of ideological purity.

The dominance of a two-party system further reinforces the challenges faced by independent voices. Structural barriers, such as ballot access restrictions and limited media coverage, make it difficult for independent candidates to gain visibility and compete on an equal footing. This creates a self-perpetuating cycle where the lack of representation discourages potential independent candidates from entering the political arena.

The decline of the political center has implications for governance, as policies become increasingly aligned with the priorities of the dominant parties. This can lead to a neglect of more nuanced solutions that may better address the complexities of certain issues. The absence of independent perspectives diminishes the diversity of thought needed for robust policy debates and decision-making.

Moreover, the vanishing center exacerbates the sense of disillusionment among voters who may find themselves ideologically adrift in a political landscape dominated by polarized rhetoric. This disenchantment can contribute to voter apathy and disengagement, as individuals feel disconnected from a system that does not adequately represent their diverse perspectives.

The media landscape also plays a role in marginalizing independent voices. News outlets often focus on the sensationalism of partisan conflicts, sidelining less sensational but more nuanced positions. This dynamic reinforces the binary narrative, shaping public discourse and influencing the perceived viability of independent candidates.

The impact of the vanishing center extends beyond policy disagreements. It affects the very essence of democratic governance, as a healthy democracy thrives on the inclusion of diverse voices and the ability to find common ground. The diminishing presence of independent voices challenges the democratic ideal of representative governance that truly reflects the diversity of public opinion.

Efforts to revitalize the political center require a multi-faceted approach. Structural reforms, such as addressing ballot access barriers and promoting fair representation, can create a more level playing field for independent candidates. Media outlets also play a crucial role; promoting unbiased reporting and providing platforms for diverse perspectives can contribute to a more inclusive political discourse.

Additionally, fostering a culture that values the complexity of issues and encourages open dialogue is essential. Citizens need to be empowered to engage critically with a spectrum of ideas, moving beyond the constraints of a binary narrative. Educational initiatives that promote political literacy and civic engagement can contribute to a more informed and discerning electorate.

The vanishing center in American politics poses challenges to the health of democratic governance. Understanding the factors contributing to the decline of independent voices and advocating for reforms that promote inclusivity are essential steps towards revitalizing the political center. A vibrant democracy requires the active participation of diverse voices, and efforts to restore the vanishing center can contribute to a more robust and representative political landscape.

The vanishing center in American politics reflects a broader shift in the dynamics of public discourse. It is not merely a consequence of electoral trends but a symptom of deeper societal changes. The polarization of media and the rise of social media echo chambers have played a pivotal role in amplifying partisan divides and marginalizing independent voices.

Social media platforms, while providing a space for individuals to express their opinions, often operate within algorithmic bubbles that reinforce pre-existing beliefs. This online polarization contributes to the fragmentation of the political center, as users are exposed to a curated stream of information that aligns with their existing views. The echo chamber effect reinforces ideological silos and further distances individuals from the diverse spectrum of perspectives that characterize a healthy political discourse.

The decline of the political center is also intertwined with the broader culture of hyper-partisanship. The "us versus them" mentality that pervades political discussions creates an environment where moderate voices are drowned out by the clamor of extreme positions. This polarization not only affects the political landscape but permeates societal interactions, contributing to divisions within communities and even families.

Furthermore, the influence of interest groups and lobbyists tends to favor well-established political parties, making it challenging for independent candidates to compete on equal footing. These interest groups often have entrenched connections with major parties, channeling financial resources and support towards candidates who align with their specific agendas. This dynamic further limits the space for independent voices that may prioritize more pragmatic and centrist solutions.

The impact of gerrymandering, the manipulation of electoral district boundaries to favor one party over another, is another layer to the complex issue of the vanishing center. Gerrymandered districts often result in the election of more extreme candidates during party primaries, as those candidates cater to the preferences of the party base. This process contributes to the ideological homogenization within parties and diminishes the influence of more moderate voices.

To address the vanishing center, it is crucial to recognize the interconnected nature of these factors. Rebuilding the political center requires not only structural reforms in the electoral system but also a cultural shift in how society consumes and engages with information. Media literacy programs, efforts to counteract gerrymandering, and campaign finance reforms are all integral components of a comprehensive strategy to restore balance to the political landscape.

Encouraging civil discourse that transcends party lines is essential. Initiatives that promote dialogue between individuals with differing political views, fostering understanding and empathy, can contribute to a more inclusive political culture. This involves breaking down the perceived barriers between left and right, recognizing shared values, and acknowledging the legitimacy of diverse perspectives.

3

THE GRIDLOCK EFFECT

Political polarization has become a defining feature of contemporary American politics, with profound implications for legislative productivity and governance. The gridlock effect, stemming from this polarization, manifests in instances where policies are strictly passed along party lines, impeding progress and perpetuating a sense of hopelessness among citizens.

One of the primary drivers of legislative gridlock is the deepening ideological divide between the left and right. Lawmakers increasingly adhere to strict party lines, viewing compromise as a betrayal of core principles rather than a necessary component of democratic governance. This entrenched partisanship often leads to legislative stalemates, as opposing factions prioritize ideological purity over the pursuit of common ground.

Instances of legislative gridlock are particularly evident during periods of divided government, where control of the executive and legislative branches is split between parties. In such scenarios, partisan differences are accentuated, making it challenging to reach bipartisan consensus on key policy issues. This dynamic was exemplified during the Obama administration, when a Republican-controlled Congress frequently clashed with the Democratic president, resulting in numerous instances of gridlock.

The gridlock effect is further exacerbated by structural factors within the political system, such as gerrymandering and the filibuster. Gerrymandered districts often produce lawmakers who cater exclusively to their party's base, disincentivizing cooperation with the opposing party. Similarly, the filibuster rule in the Senate allows a minority of senators to obstruct legislation, leading to increased gridlock and frustration among citizens.

The consequences of legislative gridlock extend far beyond stalled policy initiatives; they erode public trust in government and undermine the effectiveness of democratic institutions. When voters perceive their elected representatives as incapable of addressing pressing issues due to partisan bickering, they become disillusioned with the political process, leading to apathy and disengagement.

Moreover, the gridlock effect has tangible impacts on the daily lives of Americans, as critical issues such as healthcare reform, infrastructure investment, and immigration policy languish in legislative limbo. The inability of Congress to pass comprehensive legislation on these issues not only hampers economic growth and social progress but also perpetuates societal divisions and exacerbates inequality.

In recent years, the gridlock effect has been particularly pronounced in areas such as healthcare and climate change, where stark ideological differences between parties have hindered meaningful reform. Despite widespread recognition of the need for action on these fronts, partisan gridlock has prevented Congress from enacting substantive policy changes, leaving critical problems unresolved.

The gridlock effect is not solely a result of ideological polarization but also reflects broader trends in political behavior and governance. Increasingly, lawmakers prioritize short-term political gains over long-term solutions, prioritizing reelection prospects and partisan loyalty over the public good. This hyper-partisan environment incentivizes obstructionism and discourages cooperation, perpetuating the cycle of gridlock.

Efforts to break the gridlock often face significant challenges, as entrenched interests and institutional barriers impede progress. Bipartisan initiatives aimed at bridging the partisan divide, such as the Problem Solvers Caucus in the House of Representatives, have struggled to gain traction in an environment dominated by party loyalty and ideological purity.

Addressing the gridlock effect requires a multifaceted approach that addresses both structural barriers and cultural norms within the political system. Structural reforms, such as redistricting reform and filibuster reform, can help mitigate the influence of partisan gerrymandering and minority obstructionism, fostering a more conducive environment for legislative compromise.

Additionally, fostering a culture of collaboration and bipartisanship among lawmakers is essential for breaking the gridlock. Encouraging dialogue and cooperation across party lines, promoting civility and respect in political discourse, and incentivizing compromise through electoral reforms can help shift the dynamics of polarization and promote legislative productivity.

Furthermore, enhancing transparency and accountability in government can help rebuild public trust and hold lawmakers accountable for their actions. By increasing transparency in the legislative process, empowering citizens to participate in decision-making, and holding elected officials to account for their voting records, we can foster a more responsive and effective democracy.

Ultimately, addressing the gridlock effect requires a collective commitment to overcoming partisan divisions and prioritizing the common good. By fostering a culture of cooperation, compromise, and accountability, we can break the cycle of gridlock and restore faith in our democratic institutions.

~ 4 ~

IMMIGRATION WOES

The issue of immigration in the United States is a multi-faceted and deeply complex topic that elicits passionate debate and presents significant challenges in finding a balanced solution. At its core, immigration policy encompasses a wide range of economic, social, and humanitarian considerations, making it one of the most contentious issues in American politics.

One of the primary challenges in addressing immigration is reconciling the competing interests and concerns of various stakeholders. On one hand, there are those who advocate for stricter immigration controls, citing concerns about national security, economic competition, and the preservation of American jobs. On the other hand, there are those who argue for more lenient immigration policies, emphasizing humanitarian considerations, economic benefits, and the historical role of immigration in shaping American society.

Finding a balanced solution that addresses these divergent perspectives while upholding American values of inclusivity, opportunity, and compassion is no easy task. Immigration policy must navigate a delicate balance between enforcing border security and protecting the rights and dignity of immigrants, many of whom are fleeing violence, persecution, or poverty in their home countries.

One of the key challenges in crafting immigration policy is the sheer complexity of the issue. Immigration encompasses a wide range of issues, including legal immigration, illegal immigration, refugee resettlement, asylum policy, border security, deportation enforcement, and pathways to citizenship. Each of these components presents its own set of challenges and trade-offs, making comprehensive reform a daunting task.

Another challenge in addressing immigration is the polarized nature of the debate, which often pits advocates of stricter immigration controls against proponents of more lenient policies. This polarization has led to legislative gridlock and political stalemate, making it difficult to enact meaningful reform that addresses the root causes of immigration challenges.

Moreover, immigration policy is deeply intertwined with broader social and economic issues, including labor market dynamics, demographic trends, income inequality, and racial disparities. Any comprehensive solution to the immigration issue must take into account these broader societal factors and strive to promote equity, opportunity, and social cohesion.

One of the most contentious aspects of the immigration debate is the issue of undocumented immigrants, who are estimated to number in the millions in the United States. Advocates for stricter immigration controls argue for increased enforcement measures and stricter penalties for those who enter the country illegally. Meanwhile, proponents of more lenient policies advocate for pathways to legalization and citizenship for undocumented immigrants, recognizing their contributions to American society and economy.

Another challenge in addressing immigration is the need to balance humanitarian concerns with national security imperatives. On one hand, there is a moral imperative to provide refuge and protection to those fleeing persecution and violence in their home countries. On the other hand, there are legitimate concerns about border security and the potential for exploitation by criminal organizations and terrorist groups.

The issue of immigration also has significant economic implications, shaping labor markets, fiscal policy, and economic growth. Immigrants play a vital role in various sectors of the economy, contributing to innovation, entrepreneurship, and workforce diversity. However, immigration also poses challenges in terms of wage competition, job displacement, and fiscal costs associated with providing public services to immigrants.

Addressing the immigration issue requires a comprehensive and holistic approach that takes into account the diverse perspectives and interests of stakeholders. This approach should prioritize border security, enforcement of immigration laws, and protection of national sovereignty, while also upholding America's values of compassion, opportunity, and inclusivity.

Moreover, any meaningful solution to the immigration issue must address the root causes of migration, including poverty, violence, and political instability in sending countries. This may require targeted foreign aid, diplomatic engagement, and multilateral cooperation to address the underlying drivers of migration and promote stability and prosperity in the region.

Additionally, immigration policy should prioritize the integration and assimilation of immigrants into American society, providing support for language acquisition, education, job training, and civic engagement. This can help foster social cohesion and strengthen the fabric of American democracy, ensuring that immigrants have the opportunity to fully contribute to and participate in their communities.

Ultimately, addressing the immigration issue requires political leadership, bipartisan cooperation, and a commitment to pragmatic solutions that uphold American values while addressing the complex realities of immigration in the 21st century. By working together to find common ground and forge consensus on immigration reform, we can build a more just, inclusive, and prosperous society for all Americans.

Let's delve deeper into the complexities of immigration by examining a specific example: the Deferred Action for Childhood Arrivals (DACA) program. DACA, established in 2012 by the Obama administration, provided temporary relief from deportation and work authorization to certain undocumented immigrants who were brought to the United States as children.

The DACA program highlighted the challenges of balancing humanitarian concerns with legal and political considerations. Often referred to as "Dreamers," these young immigrants grew up in the United States and considered it their home, despite lacking legal status. DACA provided them with a measure of stability and opportunity, allowing them to pursue education, employment, and other life goals.

However, DACA also faced legal and political challenges, exemplifying the broader complexities of immigration policy. Critics of the program argued that it circumvented existing immigration laws and incentivized illegal immigration by offering a pathway to legal status for those who entered the country unlawfully. Some opponents viewed DACA as an overreach of executive authority, arguing that immigration policy should be determined by Congress rather than the president.

The legal status of DACA recipients remained uncertain, as the program faced legal challenges and attempts to repeal or rescind it by the Trump administration. The uncertainty surrounding DACA highlighted the precarious situation faced by undocumented immigrants, whose lives and livelihoods were subject to the whims of shifting political winds.

The DACA debate also underscored the human impact of immigration policy decisions, with Dreamers and their families caught in the crossfire of partisan politics. For many Dreamers, the United States was the only home they knew, and the prospect of deportation to a foreign country was a source of profound fear and uncertainty.

Despite the challenges and uncertainties surrounding DACA, the program also sparked a national conversation about immigration reform and the need for a more compassionate and pragmatic approach to immigration policy. Advocates for DACA recipients highlighted their contributions to American society and economy, emphasizing the moral imperative of providing them with a pathway to legal status and citizenship.

The DACA example illustrates the complexities of immigration policy and the challenges of finding a balanced solution that addresses the concerns of both sides. It underscores the need for comprehensive immigration reform that takes into account the diverse perspectives and interests of stakeholders, while upholding American values of inclusivity, opportunity, and compassion.

Ultimately, the DACA program served as a microcosm of the broader immigration debate in the United States, highlighting the human stories behind the policy discussions and underscoring the urgent need for bipartisan cooperation and pragmatic solutions. By learning from the experiences of DACA recipients and engaging in constructive dialogue, policymakers can work together to address the complexities of immigration and forge a more just and inclusive immigration system for the future.

5

THE INFLATION PREDICAMENT

The issue of inflation, or the general increase in prices of goods and services over time, is a pervasive economic phenomenon that can have significant impacts on the daily lives of ordinary citizens.

Inflation erodes the purchasing power of money, leading to a decrease in the real value of wages and savings, and contributing to economic strain for individuals and households.

One of the most immediate impacts of inflation is felt by consumers in their day-to-day expenses. As prices rise, households may find that their budgets are stretched thinner, forcing them to cut back on discretionary spending or make sacrifices in other areas of their lives. This can lead to reduced standards of living and increased financial stress for many families.

Rising inflation can also have a profound impact on specific sectors of the economy. For example, industries that rely heavily on raw materials or energy inputs may face increased production costs, which can lead to higher prices for goods and services. Similarly, businesses may pass on these higher costs to consumers in the form of price hikes, further exacerbating inflationary pressures.

Inflation can also have implications for housing markets, as rising prices make it more difficult for individuals and families to afford homeownership or rental housing. Inflationary pressures can drive up the cost of construction materials and labor, making new housing construction more expensive and exacerbating existing shortages of affordable housing in many areas.

Moreover, inflation can affect the ability of individuals to save and plan for the future. As the value of money declines over time, savers may find that their savings are eroded by inflation, leading to a loss of purchasing power and diminished financial security. This can be particularly problematic for retirees and individuals on fixed incomes who rely on savings to support themselves in retirement.

Inflation can also have broader macroeconomic consequences, affecting interest rates, investment decisions, and overall economic growth. Central banks may respond to rising inflation by tightening monetary policy, raising interest rates to curb inflationary pressures. Higher interest rates can increase borrowing costs for businesses and consumers, leading to reduced investment and consumption, and potentially slowing economic growth.

Furthermore, inflation can have distributional effects, impacting different groups within society unequally. For example, inflation tends to disproportionately affect low-income households, who spend a larger share of their income on essential goods and services that are subject to price increases. This can exacerbate income inequality and contribute to social unrest and political instability.

An example of the impact of inflation on daily life can be seen in the rising cost of groceries. As prices for food items such as meat, dairy, and produce increase, households may find that their grocery bills are higher, making it more difficult to afford nutritious meals for themselves and their families. This can lead to food insecurity and exacerbate health disparities, particularly for vulnerable populations such as children and the elderly.

Inflation can also affect the cost of healthcare, as rising prices for medical services and prescription drugs put additional strain on individuals and families already struggling to afford healthcare. Higher healthcare costs can lead to delays in seeking medical treatment, reduced access to essential services, and increased financial burden for patients.

Moreover, inflation can impact transportation costs, as rising fuel prices drive up the cost of gasoline and public transportation fares. This can make it more expensive for individuals to commute to work or travel for leisure, further squeezing household budgets and reducing discretionary spending.

Inflationary pressures can also affect the cost of education, as rising tuition and fees make it more difficult for students and their families to afford college or vocational training. Higher education costs can lead to increased student debt and financial hardship for graduates, limiting their ability to pursue career opportunities or invest in other areas of their lives.

Furthermore, inflation can have psychological effects on individuals and households, leading to feelings of uncertainty, anxiety, and stress about the future. As prices rise and purchasing power declines, individuals may feel less confident about their financial security and ability to meet their needs, leading to reduced consumer confidence and economic activity.

In conclusion, inflation is a pervasive economic phenomenon that can have profound impacts on the daily lives of ordinary citizens. Rising prices erode the purchasing power of money, leading to increased financial strain for individuals and households across various sectors of the economy. Addressing inflation requires a comprehensive approach that considers both macroeconomic factors and the needs of vulnerable populations, ensuring that policies are in place to support economic stability and shared prosperity for all.

6

SOARING INTEREST RATES

High-interest rates have profound implications for individuals, businesses, and the overall economy, impacting everything from borrowing costs to consumer spending and investment decisions.

When interest rates soar, the cost of borrowing money rises, making it more expensive for individuals and businesses to access credit and finance their activities.

For individuals, high-interest rates can have a significant impact on their financial well-being. Mortgage rates, for example, often track movements in interest rates, meaning that higher interest rates can result in higher monthly mortgage payments for home-owners. This can put additional strain on household budgets and make it more difficult for individuals to afford homeownership or refinance existing mortgages.

Similarly, high-interest rates can affect the cost of other forms of consumer credit, such as credit cards, auto loans, and personal loans. As interest rates rise, the cost of servicing debt increases, leading to higher monthly payments and potentially reducing disposable income available for other expenses. This can lead to reduced consumer spending, which can have ripple effects throughout the economy.

Moreover, high-interest rates can impact savings and investment decisions for individuals. While higher interest rates may lead to higher returns on savings accounts and other interest-bearing investments, they can also make it more expensive for individuals to borrow money to invest in assets such as real estate or stocks. This can affect investment decisions and asset prices, leading to increased volatility in financial markets.

For businesses, high-interest rates can pose challenges in terms of financing and investment. Higher borrowing costs can increase the cost of capital for businesses, making it more expensive to fund expansions, acquisitions, or new projects. This can lead to reduced investment and slower economic growth, as businesses may delay or scale back investment plans in response to higher interest rates.

Additionally, high-interest rates can affect the cost of servicing existing debt for businesses, particularly those with variable-rate loans or bonds. As interest rates rise, the cost of servicing debt increases, potentially putting additional strain on corporate balance sheets and limiting financial flexibility. This can lead to credit downgrades, higher borrowing costs, and increased risk of default for businesses with high levels of debt.

Furthermore, high-interest rates can impact the cost of capital for startups and small businesses, which may rely heavily on borrowing to fund their operations. Higher borrowing costs can make it more difficult for these businesses to access credit or secure financing, limiting their ability to grow and create jobs. This can have negative implications for entrepreneurship, innovation, and economic dynamism.

An example of the impact of high-interest rates on individuals can be seen in the housing market. When interest rates soar, mortgage rates rise, making it more expensive for individuals to buy homes or refinance existing mortgages. This can lead to reduced demand for housing and slower home price appreciation, as potential buyers are priced out of the market or choose to delay purchasing decisions.

Moreover, high-interest rates can affect consumer confidence and spending patterns, as individuals may become more cautious about making major purchases or taking on additional debt. This can lead to reduced demand for goods and services, which can have negative implications for businesses across various sectors of the economy. Reduced consumer spending can also lead to lower corporate profits and slower economic growth, as businesses adjust to weaker demand conditions.

In addition to impacting individuals and businesses, high-interest rates can have broader macroeconomic consequences. Central banks often raise interest rates to combat inflationary pressures or stabilize financial markets, which can lead to tighter monetary conditions and slower economic growth. Higher interest rates can also lead to appreciation of the domestic currency, making exports more expensive and reducing competitiveness in global markets.

Furthermore, high-interest rates can exacerbate income inequality, as higher borrowing costs disproportionately affect low-income households and small businesses. These groups may have limited access to credit or face higher borrowing costs due to factors such as creditworthiness or collateral requirements. This can widen the gap between rich and poor and limit economic mobility for vulnerable populations.

Addressing the consequences of high-interest rates requires a multifaceted approach that considers both short-term economic conditions and long-term structural factors. In the short term, policymakers may implement measures to support individuals and businesses affected by high-interest rates, such as targeted fiscal stimulus or monetary policy accommodation. This can help mitigate the immediate impact of higher borrowing costs and support economic activity during periods of adjustment.

In the longer term, policymakers may pursue policies to address underlying factors driving high-interest rates, such as inflationary pressures or structural imbalances in the economy. This may involve measures to promote price stability, strengthen financial regulation, or enhance productivity and competitiveness. By addressing these underlying factors, policymakers can help create a more stable and resilient economic environment that supports sustainable growth and prosperity for all.

7

HOUSING UNAFFORDABILITY

The housing crisis in the United States has reached alarming levels, with skyrocketing house prices making homeownership increasingly unattainable for the average American. This crisis has profound implications for individuals and families, affecting everything from financial stability to social mobility and community well-being. Understanding the factors contributing to housing unaffordability is essential for developing effective strategies to address this pressing issue.

One major factor contributing to housing unaffordability is the imbalance between supply and demand. Over the past few decades, demand for housing has consistently outstripped supply, leading to upward pressure on prices. This imbalance has been exacerbated by factors such as population growth, urbanization, and restrictive zoning regulations that limit the construction of new housing units.

Another contributing factor is the lack of affordable housing options, particularly in high-demand urban areas. As house prices have soared, rental prices have also risen, making it increasingly difficult for low- and middle-income households to find affordable housing. This has led to a growing affordability gap, with many individuals and families struggling to find housing that meets their needs and budget.

Furthermore, stagnant wages and income inequality have compounded the affordability crisis, as many individuals and families simply cannot afford to pay the high prices demanded by the housing market. This has led to a situation where essential workers such as teachers, nurses, and first responders are priced out of the communities they serve, leading to social and economic consequences for both individuals and society as a whole.

An example of the housing crisis can be seen in cities like San Francisco and New York, where sky-high prices have made homeownership virtually impossible for all but the wealthiest individuals. In these cities, even modest homes can sell for millions of dollars, putting them out of reach for the average American worker.

As a result, many individuals and families are forced to rent, leading to a shortage of affordable rental housing and exacerbating the affordability crisis.

Moreover, speculative investment in the housing market has contributed to the affordability crisis, as investors seek to profit from rising prices by purchasing properties and flipping them for a quick profit. This has led to inflated prices and increased competition for housing, further squeezing out low- and middle-income households.

Additionally, racial disparities in homeownership have worsened the affordability crisis, as communities of color face systemic barriers to accessing affordable housing. Discriminatory lending practices, redlining, and housing segregation have all contributed to disparities in homeownership rates, with communities of color disproportionately affected by the affordability crisis.

Addressing the housing crisis requires a multifaceted approach that addresses both supply and demand-side factors. On the supply side, increasing the supply of affordable housing through initiatives such as incentivizing the construction of affordable housing units, relaxing zoning restrictions, and providing subsidies for developers can help alleviate the affordability crisis.

On the demand side, policies that support access to homeownership for low- and middle-income households, such as down payment assistance programs, low-interest mortgage loans, and targeted tax incentives, can help make homeownership more attainable. Additionally, addressing income inequality and stagnant wages through measures such as increasing the minimum wage and expanding access to affordable healthcare and education can help improve the overall affordability of housing.

Furthermore, addressing systemic barriers to homeownership for communities of color is essential for promoting equity and social justice in the housing market. This may involve measures such as combating discriminatory lending practices, investing in affordable housing in historically marginalized communities, and promoting inclusive zoning policies that foster diverse and inclusive neighborhoods.

An example of successful affordable housing solutions can be seen in cities like Minneapolis, where policymakers have implemented initiatives to increase the supply of affordable housing and promote equitable access to homeownership. Through measures such as zoning reform, tax incentives for developers, and targeted investment in affordable housing, Minneapolis has made significant strides in addressing the affordability crisis and promoting inclusive growth.

Ultimately, addressing the housing crisis requires a comprehensive and coordinated effort from policymakers, developers, community organizations, and other stakeholders. By implementing a range of strategies that address both supply and demand-side factors, we can work together to create a more equitable, inclusive, and affordable housing market that meets the needs of all Americans.

8

CRUMBLING INFRASTRUCTURE

The state of American infrastructure, particularly aging airports and crumbling public infrastructure, is a pressing issue with significant implications for daily life and economic productivity. Across the country, infrastructure systems are showing signs of wear and tear, with many airports, roads, bridges, and public buildings in need of repair or replacement.

One of the most visible examples of crumbling infrastructure is America's aging airports. Many airports across the country are outdated and overcrowded, lacking the capacity to handle the growing number of passengers and flights. This has led to long wait times, flight delays, and a poor passenger experience for travelers. Additionally, aging airport infrastructure poses safety risks and hampers the ability of airports to attract airlines and maintain competitive airfares.

For example, LaGuardia Airport in New York City is notorious for its aging infrastructure and outdated facilities. The airport's terminals are cramped and congested, with inadequate amenities for passengers. The airport's runways and taxiways are also in need of repair, leading to frequent delays and disruptions for travelers. As a result, LaGuardia has consistently ranked among the worst airports in the country in terms of passenger satisfaction and overall quality of service.

Similarly, Chicago's O'Hare International Airport faces significant challenges due to its aging infrastructure. The airport's terminals are outdated and overcrowded, with limited seating, dining options, and amenities for passengers. The airport's runways and taxiways are also in need of repair, leading to delays and safety concerns for travelers. Despite being one of the busiest airports in the world, O'Hare has struggled to keep up with the growing demand for air travel, leading to frustration among passengers and airlines alike.

Moreover, America's crumbling public infrastructure extends beyond airports to include roads, bridges, water systems, and public buildings. Many roads and bridges are in need of repair or replacement, posing safety risks for motorists and impeding the flow of goods and services. Similarly, water systems in many cities are outdated and in disrepair, leading to water main breaks, leaks, and contamination issues.

An example of crumbling public infrastructure can be seen in the city of Flint, Michigan, where residents were exposed to lead-contaminated water due to aging and inadequate water infrastructure. The city's water system was in such disrepair that it leached lead from aging pipes into the drinking water supply, leading to a public health crisis and widespread outrage. The Flint water crisis highlighted the urgent need for investment in America's aging infrastructure and the consequences of neglecting essential public services.

Furthermore, America's crumbling infrastructure has significant economic implications, impacting productivity, competitiveness, and quality of life. Delays and disruptions caused by aging infrastructure can result in increased costs for businesses, lost productivity for workers, and reduced economic growth for communities. Additionally, inadequate infrastructure can deter investment and development, limiting job creation and economic opportunity.

For example, the American Society of Civil Engineers (ASCE) estimates that the United States faces a $2.6 trillion infrastructure investment gap over the next decade. This gap includes funding needed to repair or replace aging infrastructure, modernize transportation systems, and improve resilience to climate change and natural disasters. Failure to address this investment gap could have dire consequences for the economy, including lost jobs, reduced GDP growth, and decreased competitiveness in the global marketplace.

Moreover, crumbling infrastructure disproportionately affects low-income and marginalized communities, exacerbating existing disparities and inequalities. These communities often lack access to basic infrastructure services such as clean water, reliable transportation, and safe housing, leading to greater health risks, economic hardship, and social isolation. Addressing the infrastructure needs of these communities is essential for promoting equity, opportunity, and social justice.

In conclusion, the state of American infrastructure, including aging airports and crumbling public infrastructure, poses significant challenges for the nation. Addressing these challenges requires bold action and substantial investment to repair, modernize, and maintain essential infrastructure systems. By investing in infrastructure, we can improve the safety, efficiency, and resilience of our transportation networks, water systems, and public buildings, and ensure a brighter future for all Americans.

9

DEBT-DRIVEN SOCIETY

The issue of credit card debt has become increasingly pervasive in society, with many individuals and households struggling
to manage high levels of debt. This phenomenon has significant

implications for financial stability, economic growth, and social well-being. Understanding the reasons behind the increasing debt levels and exploring potential policy solutions is essential for addressing this pressing issue.

One reason behind the increasing levels of credit card debt is the ease of access to credit. In recent years, financial institutions have made it easier than ever for consumers to obtain credit cards, often with high credit limits and low introductory interest rates. This has led to a culture of overspending and reliance on credit, as consumers may be tempted to use credit cards to finance purchases they cannot afford with cash.

For example, many credit card companies offer rewards programs and cash-back incentives to encourage consumers to use their cards for everyday purchases. While these perks can be enticing, they can also incentivize excessive spending and lead to higher levels of debt. Additionally, the prevalence of online shopping and mobile payment apps has made it easier for consumers to make impulse purchases without considering the long-term consequences.

Moreover, stagnant wages and rising living costs have contributed to the reliance on credit cards to make ends meet. Many individuals and families struggle to cover basic expenses such as housing, healthcare, and education with their stagnant incomes, leading them to turn to credit cards as a temporary solution to bridge the gap. This can result in a cycle of debt, as individuals may struggle to pay off their balances and end up accruing interest charges and late fees.

An example of the impact of stagnant wages and rising living costs on credit card debt can be seen in the housing market. As housing prices have soared in many cities across the country, homeownership has become increasingly unattainable for the average American. Many individuals and families are forced to rent, leading to higher housing costs and reduced disposable income available for other expenses. In turn, this can lead to increased reliance on credit cards to cover essential expenses, further exacerbating debt levels.

Furthermore, the prevalence of predatory lending practices and deceptive marketing tactics has contributed to the increasing levels of credit card debt. Some financial institutions target vulnerable populations, such as low-income individuals and students, with high-interest credit cards and subprime lending products. These products often come with hidden fees, exorbitant interest rates, and aggressive debt collection practices, trapping consumers in a cycle of debt from which it is difficult to escape.

Addressing the issue of credit card debt requires a multifaceted approach that addresses both individual and systemic factors. On an individual level, financial education and literacy programs can help consumers make informed decisions about credit card use and develop responsible spending habits. Additionally, debt counseling services and financial coaching programs can provide support and guidance to individuals struggling with debt.

On a systemic level, policymakers can implement regulations and consumer protections to prevent predatory lending practices and ensure that financial institutions are transparent and accountable in their dealings with consumers. This may include measures such as capping interest rates and fees, prohibiting deceptive marketing practices, and strengthening consumer rights and protections.

Moreover, policies that address the underlying causes of debt, such as stagnant wages and rising living costs, are essential for promoting financial stability and reducing reliance on credit cards.

This may involve measures such as increasing the minimum wage, expanding access to affordable healthcare and education, and implementing policies to promote economic growth and job creation.

An example of successful policy intervention to address credit card debt can be seen in Australia, where the government implemented reforms to regulate credit card lending practices and protect consumers from predatory behavior. These reforms included measures such as capping credit card interest rates, prohibiting excessive fees and charges, and requiring financial institutions to assess the creditworthiness of borrowers before issuing credit cards. As a result, Australia has seen a decline in credit card debt levels and improved financial stability for consumers.

In conclusion, the issue of credit card debt is a pervasive and complex problem with far-reaching implications for individuals, families, and society as a whole. Addressing this issue requires a comprehensive approach that addresses both individual behaviors and systemic factors. By promoting financial literacy, implementing consumer protections, and addressing the underlying causes of debt, we can help individuals regain financial stability and build a more resilient and equitable society.

~ 10 ~

CHARTING A PATH FORWARD

In the final chapter of this book, we confront the challenges facing America and offer a vision for a more united and solution-oriented future. As we have explored throughout this journey, the political landscape is marked by division and polarization, hindering progress and perpetuating gridlock. However, despite these challenges, there is hope for a brighter future built on cooperation, dialogue, and citizen engagement.

One of the key strategies for charting a path forward is fostering bipartisan cooperation. In recent years, political polarization has made it increasingly difficult for lawmakers to work across party lines and find common ground on important issues. However, bipartisan cooperation is essential for addressing the pressing challenges facing the nation, from healthcare and immigration to climate change and economic inequality.

An example of successful bipartisan cooperation can be seen in the passage of the Affordable Care Act (ACA) in 2010. Despite significant partisan opposition, lawmakers from both parties came together to pass comprehensive healthcare reform aimed at expanding access to affordable healthcare for millions of Americans. While the ACA has faced criticism and challenges since its passage, it stands as a testament to the power of bipartisan cooperation in tackling complex issues.

Another strategy for charting a path forward is encouraging dialogue between political factions. In today's hyper-partisan environment, meaningful dialogue has become increasingly rare, with many Americans retreating into ideological echo chambers and demonizing those with opposing views. However, dialogue is essential for understanding different perspectives, finding common ground, and building consensus on solutions to shared problems.

An example of productive dialogue can be seen in the recent efforts to reform the criminal justice system. Lawmakers from both parties have come together to address issues such as mass incarceration, sentencing reform, and police accountability, recognizing the need for bipartisan solutions to improve the fairness and effectiveness of the criminal justice system. By engaging in constructive dialogue, policymakers have been able to bridge ideological divides and make progress on an issue of critical importance to the nation.

Furthermore, addressing the pressing issues facing the nation requires active citizen engagement. In a democracy, the power ultimately lies with the people, and it is up to citizens to hold elected officials accountable, advocate for meaningful change, and participate in the democratic process. Whether through voting, community organizing, or grassroots activism, citizen engagement is essential for shaping a brighter future for America.

An example of the power of citizen engagement can be seen in the recent youth-led movement for gun control reform. In the wake of tragic school shootings, young people across the country have mobilized to demand action from lawmakers, organizing marches, rallies, and advocacy campaigns to raise awareness about the need for common-sense gun laws. Their efforts have brought national attention to the issue and put pressure on elected officials to take meaningful action to address gun violence.

As we chart a path forward, it is important to recognize that the challenges facing America are complex and multifaceted. There are no easy solutions or quick fixes, but by working together, engaging in dialogue, and staying committed to our shared values, we can overcome division and build a more united and prosperous nation for future generations.

In conclusion, the future of America depends on our ability to come together, bridge our differences, and work towards common goals. By fostering bipartisan cooperation, encouraging dialogue, and empowering citizen engagement, we can chart a path forward towards a brighter and more inclusive future for all Americans.

Together, we can build a stronger, more resilient, and more united nation that reflects the best of who we are as a people.